Anne Duval

CW01024324

How to Become a Veterinary

A Complete Guide to Discover the Veterinary Career.

History, Types of Vets, Features, Study courses and Training,

to Realize the Dream of Cure the Animals

Copyright © 2020 publishing.

All rights reserved.

Author: Anne Duval

No part of this publication may be reproduced, distributed or transmitted in any form or by any means, including photocopying recording or other electronic or mechanical methods or by any information storage and retrieval system without the prior written permission of the publisher, except in the case of brief quotation embodies in critical reviews and certain other non-commercial uses permitted by copyright law.

Table of Contents

Chapter One

History of Veterinarians

Modern veterinarians assume a significant job inside the wellbeing and prosperity of our pets, additionally as steers and wild animals. Veterinarians are specialists in animal Health Sciences and advance general wellbeing by recognizing and fighting irresistible Zoonoses, which will be transmitted from animals to people. Advances in life science have furnished veterinary experts with best in class hardware, tests, strategies, and meds to treat our pets. Be that as it may, the historical backdrop of medication goes a long way past what is regularly comprehended.

The principal individuals known to be engaged with medication started around 9000 BC. in Middle Eastern nations, including Saudi Arabia, Egypt, Iran, Turkey, and Iraq. The sheep had a surmised comprehension of the clinical aptitudes want to treat their canines and different animals. From 4000 to 3000 BC, the Egyptians procured past clinical abilities and gained further ground. Egyptian chronicled reports and pictographs demonstrate how they utilized herbs to treat and advance great animal wellbeing.

Vedic writing, composed around 1500 BC, alludes to four sacrosanct writings of India composed inside the Sanskrit language that shapes the possibility of the Hindu religion. The Kahun Papyrus of Egypt goes back to 1900 BC. The two writings are most likely the fundamentally composed reports of medication. One among the hallowed writings reports the essential Indian Buddhist King, Asoka, who asserted that there had been two sorts of prescriptions: one for people and one for animals. On the off chance that he felt that there had been no meds accessible for both, he requested the restorative herbs to be purchased and planted where they were required.

The Kahun papyrus is the most seasoned known clinical content of the papyrus. It's isolated into 34 sections on explicit subjects. One of the subjects is that the gynecology of animals. The drawings of the tombs going before Kahun's papyrus for a few thousand years archive the Egyptian comprehension of gynecology. Prepared masters have experienced maternity specialists and delegated " guardian of cattle." They were blamed for Livestock Research, investment in pregnancies, and, subsequently, the introduction of calves to ensure their wellbeing and endurance.

Archeologists have discovered sections of a papyrus that was found around 1850 BC. A manual of the specialist was, which shows that the Egyptians were familiar with the life systems of animals, prepared to perceive the antecedents of certain ailments, hounds, feathered creatures, fish, and cows, and thusly the utilization of explicit medicines to influence them. The Romans, Greeks, Babylonians, Hindus, Arabs, and Jews likewise rehearsed animal medication. An individual named Urlugaledinna, who lived in Mesopotamia in 3000 BC., was viewed as a specialist in his capacity to stress for animals. Around 500 V. Chr. He dismembered a Greek researcher named Alcmaeon animals to audit them.

The primary endeavors to oversee and arrange the treatment of animals were essentially pointed toward ponies because of their financial significance to society. Inside the Middle Ages, Farri consolidated his horseshoe business with the general Horseshoe doctorate. At the point when the city hall leader of London, who varies from the chairman of London, understood that the little consideration ponies that London got in 1356, he convinced all lighters inside a seven-mile range of the town to make a decent to upgrade and manage the way they treated ponies. The corporate-prompted the creation in 1674 of the darling Farri organization.

The main school was established in Lyon, France, in 1761 by Claude Bourgelat, and it had been then that the calling of medication authoritatively started. The varsity concentrated on the investigation of the life structures and maladies of sheep, ponies, and dairy cattle with the point of fighting the passing of steers by pestilence in France. Dairy cattle ulcers were basic since forever; however, endeavored to discover the best approach to battle microorganisms needed to go to for the innovation of the magnifying lens inside the 90s. The essential ox-like immunizations were created in 1712 and were wont to annihilate a scourge in Europe.

Over the consequent ten years, veterinary schools are built up in Germany, Sweden, and Denmark. In 1791, the London Veterinary College was established and built up the historical backdrop of medication to a learned level committed to medication. The prosperity and wellbeing of ponies are their first objective for quite a long time, considering the use of ponies inside the military. At last, they concentrated on dairy cattle and different animals, and inside the end, they included pooches and different animals.

The primary school inside us was the Philadelphia Veterinary College in 1852. The University of Pennsylvania School of medication was established in 1883. The American Veterinary Medical Association (AVMA) established in 1863, and along these lines, the Bureau of Animal Industry, under the USDA, was established in 1884 and worked until 1900. The point was to monitor the overall population against irresistible ailments by killing contaminated meat, annihilating animal maladies, and improving the standard of domesticated animals.

Different Types of Veterinarians

Numerous people realize they might want to turn into a veterinarian, yet some don't understand the various sorts of animals with whom they could collaborate. A veterinarian isn't confined to treating for individuals' pets; they can work with littler, or considerably bigger animals. Now and then, they work with animals that can't be kept as pets. There are roughly six distinct sorts of vets: little animal experts, fascinating veterinarian, huge animal veterinarian, natural life veterinarian, claim to fame veterinarian, and research veterinarian.

A little animal expert is the most widely recognized; these experts work with household pets and littler well-evolved creatures. While some decide to concentrate explicitly on felines and pooches, others extend the range to incorporate bunnies, guinea pigs, and ferrets.

Intriguing veterinarians, for the most part, treat animals that aren't the run of the mill household pets, for example, felines and mutts. A few animals these experts will work with incorporate reptiles, hedgehogs, winged creatures, prairie mutts, and chinchillas. As the populace is consistently expanding its bizarre pet choice, colorful professionals are bound to be popular.

Enormous animal veterinarians will frequently end up on ranches, or different regions where domesticated animals are the principle populace. While all veterinarians must avoid potential risks while working with animals, treating bigger animals can be particularly dangerous. If an animal advances or steps onto the expert's foot, or abruptly gets frightened or apprehensive, genuine harm might be finished. Animals that ordinarily fall into the domesticated animal's classification incorporate sheep, steers, ponies, goats, pigs, and chickens.

An untamed life veterinarian works with wild animals. These animals might be found in like manner lush regions in the U.S., or may have been shipped from the fields of Africa. Experts right now may look for employment at zoological social orders, untamed life recovery focuses, or flying creature asylums. These experts generally decide to rehearse inside a specific territory, so understanding the animal and flying creature species in their given area will be very gainful.

Forte veterinarians, despite everything, work with animals, however, in an increasingly engaged field. For example, these people may decide to become dental specialists, ophthalmologists, or cardiologists, just for animals. Animal types may likewise be picked, for example, an avian vet (winged animals), or an equine vet (ponies and jackasses).

An examination veterinarian will work in a lab setting, investigating pathology, biomedical research, and microbiology, among others. These people are answerable for looking into animal-related medical issues, for example, the West Nile Virus and Mad Cow Disease. The most well-known work environment for these people is government or state-run organizations.

During instruction, certain hands-on necessities must be satisfied. While entry-level positions and practice in the field are generally required, supervision is regularly required before a veterinarian is sufficiently qualified to perform assignments all alone.

These veterinary professionals must hold a four-year certification in an important field and a doctoral qualification before opening their own training or entering this field. A Doctor of Veterinary Medicine may not be the main necessity for certain people. For the individuals who wish to analyze and treat animals discovered distinctly in the wild, or other explicit living spaces, travel to different nations or broad time spent at a zoo might be required. Declarations and extra preparation may likewise help veterinarians to increase propelled practice, or give evidence of an individual's information and ability in a specific specialization.

Most people are familiar with the standard type of medicine commonly called "pet veterinary," but the industry can be diverse that has many specialties. If you are considering this line of work, or if you are an animal lover who needs the services of a more specialized professional, consider the following types of positions that fall into this field of drugs.

Pet doctor: this is often the standard neighborhood doctor for dogs and cats. He is also the best known of the profession. Why cats and dogs, you ask? These are the most common types of animals. Most animal veterinarians also see typical animals like rabbits, hamsters, gerbils, guinea pigs, and ferrets, but if you prefer more exotic companions like lizards, snakes or spiders (Oh, my), then you will ask your district doctor about your credentials and preferences for treating these animals. Generally, canines and felines are the expected patients in these facilities.

The veterinary exotic: this professional is often found working in zoos, refuges, or circuses, but he or she may also be in the business of dealing with these pets is not typical of the above such as lizards, or perhaps monkeys that some people may legally have in their homes.

Wildlife doctor: these qualified animal doctors probably do not run private farms, as they are in the field of animal management for conservation purposes. They will work for state or wildlife shelters or reserves to label wildlife for Studies, control extinction, persistence in habitat, etc. they are also used in the field of research on topics such as animal behavior and animal control.

Equine veterinarian: these can also be the owners of local enterprises, and even if they treat and care for all standard pets, they need special certifications for livestock. You will be ready to inaugurate individual animals in facilities equipped for vaccinations, vaccinations, checks, and examinations, but the doctor will also generally be familiar with the trip to your farm, field or barn to provide services. These doctors can also work for agencies specializing in the internal control of livestock or the product of raw materials.

Doctor of Marine life: in fact, these doctors work in areas that host aquatic animals such as the coast or the zoo. Redfish do not need to be applied.

If you are looking to find a care provider for your pet, your typical veterinarian will be. Other frequently frequented types of animal professionals treat livestock such as cows, horses, sheep, or perhaps turkeys, and therefore the qualifications of the local veterinarian should be readily available to customers.

Starting A Career As A Veterinarian

The veterinarians who work in clinical settings practice medicine in specific fields, such as PET or PET medicine, medicine, reptile Medicine, ratite Medicine, livestock Medicine, equine, Sport, race track, show, and rodeo, or laboratory medicine while other veterinarians work in research fields of human medicine, veterinary medicine, and pharmacology.

This study has made an important contribution to the isolation of oncoviruses, Salmonella species, Brucella species, and various other pathogens. They also helped overcome malaria and yellow fever, solved the mystery of botulism, produced an anticoagulant for the treatment of heart disease, and developed new and advanced surgical techniques for humans, such as hip replacement and limb and organ transplants.

Ethical

Like other health professionals, veterinarians also need serious ethical decisions regarding patients in their care. There has always been a discussion or controversy about procedures such as Cat-clearing, Dog-Tail, earring, and holding dogs. In some countries, such procedures are considered illegal, thus putting an end to their practice. The Association of veterinary doctors adopted the veterinary oath in July 1969, which was amended by the board of AVMA in November 1999, according to which veterinarians must respect strict medical ethics comparable to that of humans.

Career options

Some veterinarians work in an area called regulatory medicine, which guarantees the country's food security by working with the USDA FSIS, or by working with the USDA APHIS to prevent the introduction of exotic animal diseases, to prevent them. The emerging area of natural medicine is even more directly involved with veterinary surgeons in health care and provides a multidisciplinary approach to medical research involving environmental scientists.

Today, veterinarians all over the world work in schools and colleges where they teach students what they need to know to succeed.

Today, many veterinarians also take educational jobs in schools and colleges, training students to obtain a veterinary diploma. Veterinary schools are higher education institutions, or part of them, participating in the training of future veterinary operators. The eligibility criteria, structure, teaching methods, and modules vary from university to university.

Necessary instruction

For example, in other states of the United States of America, and a doctorate in veterinary medicine (D. V. M.) in three years, in Pennsylvania, the degree is awarded after a four-year program. It usually consists of a classroom course followed by clinical practice. Currently, unlike schools or universities of human medicine, a follow-up traineeship or residence is not required but is optional for those who opt for additional training and accreditation.

Surprisingly, the number of veterinarians who have internships and/or residences is increasing as a result of growing demand in rural areas. Admission to these veterinary schools or colleges is very competitive, and access to a medical or judicial School in the United States is easier than obtaining a veterinary university. This is because there are few veterinary faculties, so the selection process is very selective. According to the Ministry of labor, only one in three candidates are admitted to a program.

Public health is another option for veterinarians. Public and private veterinarians, diagnostic, and screening laboratories. Some veterinarians are also state epidemiologists, environmental health directors, and directors of public health services of the state and the city. The army also points to taking care of animals in their department.

This profession is gaining popularity as a result of the demand for a wide range of treatments and services needed for animals and humans.

THINGS YOU NEED TO KNOW PRIOR TO STARTING VETERINARIAN TRAINING

To become a certified veterinarian, you need to know what kind of education and training is needed. First, you must complete a 4-year degree, where ideally, you will focus on sciences (such as biology, chemistry, Animal Sciences, and mathematics). If you obtain a degree with a GPA 3.5 or higher and have a solid scientific background, this will increase your chances of being accepted into an accredited veterinary school and eventually earning your doctorate in Veterinary Medicine.

Important tips:

It is also useful to work or volunteer in animal-related jobs, which will make you a more desirable candidate for veterinary schools.

The Postgraduate School usually takes about four years to complete and will include practical veterinary experience with animals. Some schools offer concurrent master's programs for those who are training to become veterinarians. With some additional courses, you can also get your master's degree in Business Administration (MBA)!

Did you know?

Look for universities that are accredited by the American Veterinary Medical Association (AVMA), as they are the leading association for veterinary professionals in the United States. After obtaining and obtaining the diploma of a doctor in veterinary medicine, you must obtain a license in the state where you plan to practice. After obtaining a license, you can work in a private clinic with small and large pets, with farm and ranch animals or similar types of animals. Alternatively, you can pursue a career in education, government, or commercial work.

In addition to the private veterinary clinics are where 2/3 of all veterinarian's work. When you are thinking of working in a field related to education, your strong Veterinary Teaching and practical training will be ideal for universities and universities that hire teachers, professors, and researchers. Educational and government institutions in the United States hire trained veterinarians to help fight animal diseases (especially those that can be shared among humans). If you want to diagnose and treat wild animals, working for a local, state, or federal job can offer you the best opportunities.

Many companies, such as farms, ranches, private research facilities, zoos, and natural habitats, have veterinarians on-site to take care of the welfare of their animals. This includes the administration of vaccines, the diagnosis of diseases and injuries, and the treatment of any problems that animals may have. These types of careers allow you to specialize in specific types of animals or types of treatment (such as surgery or anesthesiology). In addition, they do not need start-up costs or commercial expertise to run their own private veterinary clinic.

The Advantages of a Career As a Veterinarian

What do you get when you are a veterinarian? Basic! If you like animals, you get the opportunity to deal with them. The upsides of being a veterinarian are the point at which you love this activity, and you simply continue going ahead, and you needed to find out additional. For the time and exertion, you have experienced during your long periods of study and training, you will get the opportunity to have the award of having a great job, get the chance to think about animals, and win cash. En route of training and investigations of being a veterinarian, it would not be simple, and you will experience extraordinary difficulties and school works. However, it is all justified, despite all the trouble when you finish such a course. In veterinarian course you will take up and complete a doctorate which is around seven or eight years of fruition, then again veterinarian expert is another course, however, just takes two years and needs to pass confirmation.

With everything considered, the incredible favorable position of being a veterinarian is that at whatever point you get the degree and finish all the prerequisites, at that point, you simply own it. At the point when a veterinarian has longer and enough experience of the activity, he/she can get the calendar she needs to, she can deal with occasions or not relying upon his/her viewpoint. She/he can take a shot at his/her own center or work in an emergency clinic. Being a veterinarian resembles being a human specialist, too; they get the opportunity to help individuals to give clinical help for their pets.

If you decide to be a piece of the military, you get the opportunity to have motivating forces, for example, extraordinary rewards and advances, and you become an official too. At the point when you resign, you will have incredible advantages for retirement with free or ease profit for certain merchandise as well as administrations.

Beside incredible compensation when a veterinarian can help and help animals, they gain satisfies and extraordinary inclination for their activity very much done, and they get the chance to see different sorts of pets that would most likely add a grin to their face. Before the day's over, they will be progressively energized of what might "tomorrow" bring them.

Once more, if a veterinarian needs to acquire more and get incredible advantages more than expected, they can pursue the military, make some train and certificates, and they are a great idea to go, be an official get paid, appreciate the activity, and when retirement comes, they simply get increasingly extraordinary motivating forces and advantages.

Becoming a Veterinarian Or Veterinarian Technician

Becoming a veterinarian or veterinarian technician (vet tech) is the long-lasting desire of numerous animal sweethearts. Accomplishing this objective is a long and testing street loaded up with physical, mental, and emotional requests. In any case, any animal darling who makes it will disclose to you it merits all the trouble.

The measure of the information held by a veterinarian is significantly more enhanced than that held by specialists of human medicine. The veterinary educational program remembers the entirety of the various species and physiologies for the animal realm. What's more, numerous vets, particularly private practice general professionals, must have the option to take on such differing duties, including that of drug specialists, specialists, diagnosticians, radiologists, behaviorists, orthopedic specialists, dental specialists, et al.

It is likewise factually progressively hard to enter and finish veterinary medicine school just because there are just 28 schools in the United States offering this coursework.

To turn into a vet, you need extraordinary evaluations in secondary school, an adoration for animals, four years of college, four years of veterinary medical school, to finish a veterinary medical board assessment and a state board assessment also. At exactly that point, can you lawfully rehearse veterinary medicine? It is an enormous time and money related to responsibility. A deep-rooted responsibility to proceeding with instruction is likewise required - remaining current on new systems, medical medications, and accessible medication treatments.

Entry-level position or residency credits are not required yet are offered to accomplish propelled capability or affirmation for a claim to fame.

Before applying for veterinary medicine school, contact your schools of decision and comprehend the scholarly prerequisites, course work, and grade necessities. It is additionally significant to have worked (in the late spring or after school) in an important field.

Becoming a veterinary technician, be that as it may, is a lot simpler. Obviously, the duties and prizes are not as fluctuated or seriously confounded, yet for somebody who doesn't have the assets to turn into a full vet, a vet tech degree can, in any case, be fulfilling and fulfilling. Vet specialists perform a considerable lot of similar obligations for a vet that a medical caretaker would for a doctor, including routine research centers and clinical methods.

They direct clinical work in private practice under the supervision of an authorized veterinarian, performing different medical tests, for example, urinalysis, inoculations, and blood draw. A certified vet tech may likewise look for some kind of employment in examine offices under the supervision of authorized vets or doctors.

A portion of the work a vet tech performs may be horrendous, physically and emotionally requesting, and conceivably hazardous. Cleaning cages and holding and lifting animals are normal. A vet tech may likewise be approached to control an animal, which dangers introduction to nibbles and scratches. The working environment can, some of the time, be uproarious and confused. The individuals who witness mishandled animals or who are asked to euthanize matured, undesirable, or miserably harmed animals may encounter emotional agony and stress.

Most section level vet specialists are required to have a 2-year partner degree from an American Veterinary Medical Association (AVMA)- licensed college program. Graduation from an AVMA-certify vet tech program qualifies understudies to take the required credentialing assessment in any state in the United States.

Becoming a Good Veterinarian

Are you looking for a career in the veterinary field? If you like the medical profession and, most importantly, love animals and want to help them, then this career can be the right one for you. But it's not so easy to get into a veterinary school. There are only 28 colleges in the United States, and, as such, it is harder for aspiring candidates to get because of the tough competition. To get into these colleges, then you do not need good grades, you need great nuances!

Important Factors

But this does not mean that you will have a chance only if you are a student. There are other factors that are important to get into these colleges. These include other activities and experiences with animals. This also includes a solid background in mathematics, science, and biology. The good news is that this area has diversified over the past two decades and, therefore, not only targets individuals of a particular status quo.

The duration of time

Four years of college and another four years of Veterinary Medicine constitute the theoretical knowledge of a veterinarian. Residency credits or traineeships are not mandatory for this grade. But if you want to get a specialty certification or advanced qualification, you should probably take these credits. A debate has raged in recent years about whether it is right for international students to take "additional veterinary residency credits."

Completion of the IFP School does not mean the beginning of the practice.

Just because you finished, the veterinary school does not mean that you became eligible for a veterinarian. There is a national examination approved by the National Veterinary Council. This is a very difficult exam and is like the lawyer exam taken in law.

The test is not completed until you pass a state examination at the council level taken by the state in which you prefer the practice. The requirements for such exams are different in different states, although there are some states that accept votes made in other states. This allows you to practice in more than one state, even if you took the exam in one state.

Advanced Level Course

If you want to be a veterinarian or a coach, you must continue to take courses throughout your life. These courses include seminars or workshops in this area. These workshops and seminars are important because they keep your individuality on the ground. They help you keep track of new systems of ideas, techniques, and diseases discovered and how to deal with them.

A good idea to keep track of these new innovations is to enroll in veterinary medicine journals that would improve your complete knowledge of the discipline.

The veterinary field is like the human medical field only that it is more complex than the human field because of the large number of species involved, so choose this field only if you are an animal enthusiast.

Chapter Two

The Qualifications Necessary to Practice Veterinary Medicine

Like humans, animals will need effective health treatment. It is common for animals to need preventive care to maintain good health and specialized therapy if they are injured or sick. Veterinary science will be essential for the study and development of animals. A veterinarian will administer diagnostic, medical, and therapeutic treatments for each type of animal.

Veterinarians provide medical assistance to livestock, pets, wildlife, and animals in laboratories, zoos, and racecourses. Some will protect people from diseases affecting animals and conduct medical research on the association involving animal and human health problems. Others will conduct preliminary research and raise public awareness about animals and Health Science. A little applied for research work and developed innovative ways to use the knowledge gained about animals. Many veterinarians diagnose a state of health in animals and advise owners of appropriate care; vaccinate animals against diseases; provide treatment to animals for infections or diseases and conduct additional medical procedures.

If you are interested in learning how to become a veterinarian, you must first understand that you need to have a doctorate in veterinary medicine from a certified college. Programs require a minimum of 45 credit hours and may require a degree. Many applicants will complete a degree program before applying to a veterinary school. Several graduate students will begin internship programs one year after graduation.

Good employment prospects are expected in the coming years, especially for veterinarians who have extensive experience in the treatment of animals and also those who have specialties. A career in veterinary medicine will be an excellent option for people who have a real desire to help and improve animal health and well-being. Future veterinarians should have effective manual skills and an ability to effectively converse with pet owners. Excellent communication and business skills will also be important for veterinarians who want to open a private practice.

A QUALIFICATION IN HIGH DEMAND

If you excel in science and love animals, then you should consider exploring veterinary training and become an expert in Animal Care. This is an area where you can not only help improve the quality of life of animals, but you can be financially rewarded for your services.

Veterinary scientists and veterinary technologists/technicians are in great demand. This should come as no surprise. Millions of people in the United States and Canada love their pets and are willing to spend money to see these animals in the best of health.

But it can be surprising that the skills acquired in veterinary training are not applied only to the care of animals. In fact, the results of research on diseases affecting animals have been applied to human medicine. After all, many diseases affect both animals and humans.

It takes a personality to become a veterinarian. It is a fact that you need to be compassionate and patient when it comes to animals. But you also need to have a strong constitution to manage the sight of bloody animals. You need to be able to make difficult decisions - decide that it is better to euthanize an animal than to try to treat it.

You also need to be interested in understanding the behavior of animals, habits, and physical systems they have. You must be physically fit to be able to lift and keep the animals as well.

Not to mention the academic requirements you must have. To enter the graduate program in veterinary science, you must excel in science and mathematics.

Another way to demonstrate an early commitment to veterinary training is to get volunteers with your local animal shelter or veterinarian. In fact, it is essential to be accepted into the Veterinary College as you show that you are committed to animal welfare outside the school as well as inside.

Before entering the Doctor of Veterinary Medicine (DVM) program, you must make sure that the program is properly accredited. There are not many colleges in the United States that offer accredited veterinary diplomas. No veterinary scientific training can be done online. So, pay attention to schools that claim to offer DVM programs online.

If you think veterinary training is not for you, consider making a certificate in one of the various aspects of Animal

Care. For example, you can make a certificate of dog obedience training or pet grooming.

These, in general, will not pay apart from having veterinary training. However, if you can provide obedience training or grooming services to an affluent clientele, you can earn money.

Licenses Required for Veterinary Careers

There are several licenses required for veterinary careers, although there are also entry-level jobs in this area. It all depends on what you want to do, how long you want to stay in school, and where you want your career for yourself. It is important to know all the requirements of your professional career before embarking on your professional career in the field of Animal Care.

If you are going to become a veterinarian, you will have to attend a serious education and complete all the necessary steps to obtain your license. You will be asked to complete a veterinary doctor from an accredited higher education institution and pass the state license examinations before you can legally establish yourself as a veterinarian. Many veterinarians choose a specialty such as Anesthesiology, dentistry, pathology, radiology, or surgery. You will then have to pass a state exam to become a veterinary technician or an authorized technologist.

If getting a doctorate sounds like too much school for you, perhaps a career as a veterinary technician or technologist is more your speed. Veterinary technicians must complete a four-year degree, and veterinary technicians must complete a two-year degree. Many universities and technical schools across the country offer accredited veterinary technology programs that include courses in anatomy, diagnostic equipment, Pharmacology, Physiology, test procedures, and more.

There are other veterinary careers that do not require a formal university education, although people working in these fields may have diplomas. Animal trainers, hairdressers, and zookeepers can start without having completed school years. However, some of these jobs require professional licenses. Hairdressers and pet keepers often complete some studies, although this type of program can be completed in just two weeks. Other veterinary work requires two, four, eight years of study, or more.

It is important to know what your options are and what you are getting involved in as you embark on the path to a veterinary career. Knowing the education and licenses required for veterinary careers is the first step in a successful career in the field of Animal Care.

The Life of a Veterinarian

How does it feel to be a veterinarian? Life as a veterinarian is rewarding but difficult and demanding, is that the answer of most veterinarians. To be a veterinarian, you want to have a passion or clinical interest in animals, have great interpersonal skills, and have a robust work ethic.

We will divide the life-style into several categories to offer readers thought of the pros and cons of being a veterinarian.

PATIENTS: ANIMALS AND THEIR HUMAN GUARDIANS

Benefit

You will work together with your passion

It is rewarding and satisfying to diagnose, treat and make animals feel better

Disadvantage

The animals will probably protest to be taken to the veterinarian's office. you'll be bitten, scratched or hit

Careless, difficult or emotional human guardians

Most people are inspired to enter veterinary science due to their love for animals. In our interviews with pre-vet students, a passion for animals or a childhood pet provided the spark to pursue a career as a veterinarian. As Amanda Wong, a student at the University of California, Berkeley, explains, "I've always had a fascination with animals from an early age and knew I wanted to pursue a career working closely with animals. The pursuit of medicine became the foremost obvious option on behalf of me soon..."

Dr. Jonathan Woodman, veterinarian, and owner of Town Country Veterinary Services share an enriching recent experience with a patient "Dolly may be a 13-year-old Dalmatian whom we treated in January and February this year. She was so sick with an intestinal virus and weakened that she couldn't even stand it. I used to be sure she wouldn't survive. I worked very hard to save lots of her, and everything seemed useless, but it finally began to return slowly. This summer, I saw that I saw her return to her normal activities and happy self, and it had been very rewarding."

Perhaps one among the foremost difficult parts of the work is that the parents of animals and human guardians accompanying patients. That's where great interpersonal skills inherit play. Animals are attacked with human guardians, like farm owners or pet parents, which may be difficult to handle. Unfortunately, the Guardians can go from irrational and unsightly to even careless. This is often a standard issue in veterinary communities.

WORK: WHAT VETERINARIANS DO

Advantages of being a veterinarian

Versatile grade with different industrial applications, daily responsibilities, and mobility

Ability to have your own practice

In animal practice, it is often an anesthesiologist, a surgeon or an obstetrician at an equivalent time, counting on the clients that the day brings you, this is often not the case with human care providers

Disadvantages of being a veterinarian

Potential exhaustion and compassion fatigue

You will see the animals within the pain and suffering of every disease and can probably perform euthanasia

Long hours within the office and on-call during weekends and in the dark

Revenue a discretionary charge for depositaries

Being a veterinarian is analogous to being a detective. "The veterinarian (s) should (should) learn to conduct insightful interviews with owners, observe and skim the visual communication of the animals, and use strong deduction and rational application of the tests to know ... the simplest action plan for animal Health," says Jennifer Livesay, a DVM student at Oklahoma State University in an interview. You'll get to be a person to try everything possible to research the disease or treatment of the injury, especially since patients can't verbalize their condition. This contrasts with human medicine, where functions like surgery or anesthesia should be mentioned, other physicians. While veterinarians refer more complicated cases to specialists, they will perform routine procedures themselves.

When most people believe becoming a veterinarian, they tend to consider a personal practice that focuses on pets. The private practice employs the bulk of 61,000 veterinarians within the labor pool, consistent with the Bureau of Labor Statistics. A doctorate in medicine (DVM) is flexible, however, and exposes a good range of career options in research, government, or business.

Depending on the sort and size of your practice, a veterinarian's hours are often exhausting. It's not uncommon for a veterinarian to take care of normal operating hours from 9: 00 to 18: 00 Monday to Friday, also as on-call just in case of emergency after opening hours and weekends. This is often amplified if there are fewer vets serving a post, and pet parents have only a couple of vets to trust. Additionally, counting on the design mode, night shifts are generally provided for ER veterinarians. For this reason, a veterinarian's work-life balance varies greatly counting on his client list and, therefore, the demand for his services.

After a short time on the bottom, veterinarians may suffer from compassionate fatigue. Compassion fatigue is typically described because the whirlwind of emotions requires an excessive amount of or insufficient. People that suffer from compassionate fatigue could also be emotionally exhausted or ready to get over the milder events to feel numb by patients and life outside of labor. It's estimated that veterinarians suffer death five times more often than human doctors, which naturally increases these conditions.

Finally, pet and animal care generally fall into discretionary income. When times are excellent, pet parents or farm owners pay for treatments. However, when the economy shrinks, funds to hide additional care are less available.

Veterinarians report that customers can delay providing medical aid to their pets to save lots of money, only to require them to a later stage where conditions have deteriorated seriously.

Is Veterinary Medicine the Right Career Choice For You?

Veterinarians - or veterinarians for short - are doctors specializing in animals. The word comes from the Latin "veterinae," which suggests"Animal Project." The term veterinary was first used in 1646 by Thomas Browne. Today, medicine includes many different careers. Some veterinarians add a clinical environment and practice pet medicine on small animals such as dogs, cats, and pets. Other veterinary scrub operators focus on livestock or production medicine, which incorporates beef and a dairy cow, sheep, pigs, and poultry also as equine medicine (racetrack, rodeo, performance Medicine). Other specialties include laboratory medicine in reptiles and rats, as well as animal surgery, general medicine, and dermatology. These latter specialties require postdoctoral training. The demographic data of veterinarians have changed dramatically over the past 25 years: until the 1980s, the percentage of male and female veterinarians has shifted significantly to men, but in recent years, women are the predominant diplomats.

Advanced veterinary certification allows some veterinarians to pursue a research career, and veterinarians make many important medical discoveries, including the isolation of oncoviruses and salmonella and Brucella species, as well as other pathogenic species. Veterinary scrub researchers have been at the forefront of the struggles against the yellow cat and malaria in the United States and are a veterinarian who first noticed the appearance of West Nile disease in New York zoo animals. The identity of the agent that causes botulism was first discovered by a veterinarian, as well as the anticoagulant used to treat human heart disease. Many human surgical techniques have been perfected for the first time in animals, such as organ and limb transplants and hip replacement.

Because in the United States, veterinary schools are often supported by the state, preference for applicants is usually given to state students, and out-of-State students have to pay a limited fee. Admission criteria vary greatly from state to state, depending on the percentage of vacancies and the number of candidates in the state. Therefore, in some states, admission to the school is often much more competitive than medical admission to the school. Even among schools in the same state, the percentage of student admissions applications can vary greatly. Studying abroad is possible, but graduates abroad are often disabled in demand for graduate education. In the United

States, admission to school generally requires scores on the GRE and MCAT or VCAT tests. The typical GRE score for veterinary students in the United States is 1350, and therefore the average is 3.5. In addition, the different veterinary schools require specific university studies, also as a broad experience related to Animals (of the order of a thousand hours or more). In North America, the school lasts four years, one of which is dedicated to clinical rotation. After passing a National Council exam, you can do an internship or residency in white jackets in the advanced areas.

As is the case with doctors in white robes for humans, Doctors With veterinary scrubs often have to make important ethical decisions regarding the care of their patients. For example, there is currently a debate in veterinary exfoliating circles about the ethics of cat declaration, about trimming and mating ears and tails, even as disheveled dogs.

The Hardest Parts of Being a Vet

Being a veterinarian is often among the most important rewarding careers in the world. We have the power to heal companions, who, for many, are part of the family. But being a veterinarian also has its share of challenges. This is this blog; I will offer you the scoop in what I feel are the three most difficult aspects of being a veterinarian.

Euthanasia

Many times, the clientele discusses how euthanasia should be the hardest part of my job. Although they are often very emotionally demanding, the reality is that euthanasia is not the most difficult part of my career. As a veterinarian, this is a double-edged sword. Euthanasia is usually an exquisite service to provide to an animal that suffers or has a terminal illness and does not have an adequate quality of life. That said, repeatedly, a Veterinarian Develops a private relationship, not only with the owners of animals but also with the animal. It is sometimes very difficult not to break and cry during euthanasia. Sometimes it happens.

Abuse

If you have ever looked into the innocent eyes of an animal that is afraid of the inexplicable of individuals, an animal that trembles thinking that could be beaten at any time for reasons that are not understood, then recognize this kind of heartbreaking calls. Cruelty to animals can occur in an additional way compared to physical violence; it can also include negligence, hoarding, and negligence to call a couple of. I regularly see cases when the owner of an animal does not even realize that he is careless about his pet. Pets believe that their owners provide not only food, water, and shelter, but also a comfortable environment. As veterinarians, we are ethically sure to report suspected cases of abuse. This alone, however, is not enough to avoid the disgusting feeling we have knowing that this is happening and seeing it first - hand in our clinics.

Missed treatment

In my opinion, the most difficult aspect of being a veterinarian has a young, mostly healthy animal with a solvable problem, but there are no resources to correct the difficulty. The reality is that even the healthiest animals can encounter unexpected diseases or accidents. That's often why I'm a big fan of pet insurance. Cat and dog insurance can often make the difference between offering care to your pet or having to choose euthanasia because of the cost alone.

Sometimes diseases and accidents for pets are often very demanding both emotionally and financially. Repeatedly, veterinarians find themselves in a situation where we think that we can cure a pet, but there are simply no funds to treat the patient. Many of us do not realize that veterinary clinics are companies, charities. Given a large amount of overhead associated with operating a hospital, many clinics have little or no financial leeway to maintain the business in positive numbers, including the donation of products and services. Too often, clients enter a veterinary clinic with the hope that no matter what they are willing to pay, their pet will receive the care it needs. As an animal lover, it is so difficult to inform someone that your pet will not receive such care. It is even more difficult to observe that the animal comes out of the door, without the medical care it needs. These circumstances leave us with a disturbing sense of helplessness and sadness. There are few things worse than knowing that a choice about life, or the norm of it, refused the money.

The Best Parts of Being a Vet

There are many rewarding aspects of being a veterinarian, relying on your personality and what motivates you. I will start with the most rewarding aspect on my behalf and then move on to a few minor aspects, including aspects that my colleagues find rewarding.

1.A. teaches other veterinarians and technicians. There is nothing more rewarding for me as a veterinarian than helping a coworking learn and master a replacement ability, whether its blood collection, positioning an IV catheter, or teaching a replacement surgery to another veterinarian. Seeing the fun in your face once you complete a task without help is amazing.

1.B., especially from the point of view of Medicine. I am surgical minded, which means I prefer " quick fixes."I.e., a broken bone - > participate in surgery, repair it. Bleeding from the spleen - > participate in surgery, remove it. A patient comes with drag, and within 12 hours, you fixed it.

Other aspects that reward counts on your work

Veterinarians are working in shelters, like to help pets in extremely poor conditions and in great need. Turning malnourished and gnawed dogs into what can often look like a completely new animal is often extremely rewarding.

Develop long-standing relationships with members of your community.

Practice ownership and start a business from scratch and absolutely nothing, in a booming respected veterinary practice. (very rewarding for business people)

Community outreach and volunteering. Of course, we need to do something to earn an income, except for a lot of giving our services, our skills and our drugs, and seeing the exceptional impact that this can have on a community that has little or no, is often extremely rewarding.

Still others in the research find a huge reward in the discovery of the latest microbes, or especially new drugs to treat certain conditions.

Chapter Three

Veterinary Assistant

The field of medicine is so vast and full of possibilities for someone with a passion for animals, domestic and wild. There has been an excellent revolution in the veterinary field, and innovations and technologies have improved the working conditions of care providers and animal health.

The role of veterinary assistants has developed more and more, and with the technology, they need to be ready to do more work. Their schools have also revised their curriculum to keep up with developments in the field, also due to the change in the role of veterinary assistants.

It is worth noting that veterinary work can sometimes be dangerous because it has to hit the animals, some of which are in trouble and, therefore, restless. However, this is a satisfying career, especially for animal lovers who can not only help sick animals but also cheer the owners of these animals. It is also a very competitive field because a little like qualifications in human medicine are vital and, therefore, the quality of treatment cannot be compromised.

Their schools offer a range of topics including animal behavior, drug treatment of animals, animal ethics and legal issues, record keeping, and animal care. At an essential introductory level, schools will offer a mix of these topics, but together, as they advance in their careers, they will be ready to perfect and focus on their field of interest.

A veterinary assistant is a veterinary doctor who a nurse is to a doctor. The training will provide you with skills and prepare you for tasks such as caring for sick and injured animals, administering medications and vaccines, grooming pets, assisting during surgery, and maintaining a record. Thanks to the stress of the profession and technological developments, most Veterinary Assistant Schools also offer training in computer and laboratory skills.

Tasks vary depending on the size and nature of the institution for which a veterinary assistant works. Most private offices focus on one type of animal, for example, a canine clinic. However, large institutions, such as research institutes and zoos, will affect several animals. Various experiences hone different skills needed to accomplish your tasks.

There are many community colleges and technical schools that offer training in veterinary assistant courses. Some veterinary assistant schools also offer online courses that allow you to continue the course at home. The advantages of continuing these hospitality courses are many. One during a position is ready " is able to review at their own pace and approach the courses in a combination that best suits them. The other is able to save a lot on tuition when studying online.

If you are looking to start a career in the veterinary field, otherwise, you are already working for a veterinary practice, but looking for certification in the veterinary assistant school Veterinary Assistant job is the best option. Theoretical and practical training will give you a competitive advantage in a profession that respects qualification and knowledge.

TOOLS AND PROGRAMS USED BY VETERINARY ASSISTANTS

There are many differences between veterinary technicians and veterinary assistants, including the tools and programs used by veterinary assistants. Training, homework, and school are different for veterinary assistants compared to veterinary technicians. Therefore, the tools and programs they use are obviously different. If you are considering becoming a veterinary assistant, it may be an honest idea to familiarize yourself with the tools and programs you will use at work before starting the training or application.

Veterinary assistants are not required to complete a two-year diploma, as are veterinary technicians, and although some assistants receive veterinary training through certificate or diploma programs, they probably have little or no training before starting this type of work.

While a veterinary technician is no longer a type of nurse, a veterinary assistant is no longer an administrative or administrative position, where most of the training is completed on the job. He is likely to be trained to use many of the most important basic veterinary tools in the examination room, although his work will likely be limited to keeping the animal motionless for controls and preparing space for examinations. You will probably also be responsible for cleaning the examination rooms and kennels after the animals are inside.

Computer programs used by veterinary assistants are among the most basic and commonly known in the professional world, such as Word, Excel, and QuickBooks. If you've never used any of these programs before, it might be an honest idea to require a core technology class in a school or technology to have public knowledge of the major common programs used in today's offices. Your other administrative tasks will likely involve answering phones, storing patient records, entering data, welcoming patients and their owners, selling products, and billing customers for services rendered.

If you want to become a veterinary assistant, you will need a high school diploma or GED, but apart from that, most jobs do not require formal training. Many employers will prefer a minimum of a certificate or the completion of certain veterinary classes, while others will be happy to train you in the workplace. In any case, it is essential to solicit as much experience as possible to work with animals and to understand what kind of tools and programs you can use while working.

THE BASICS OF VETERINARY ASSISTANT DEGREE PROGRAMS

If you graduate from one of the accredited veterinary assistant programs of your state of study, you will have a good job prospect that awaits you after graduation. It is a job that involves working with veterinarians in animal hospitals, clinics, and laboratories. As a veterinary assistant, you will play a vital role in the veterinarian's office to perform essential tasks such as administering medicines, bathing animals, feeding animals, and general assistance with the daily activities of the veterinary team.

What will you learn in a veterinary assistant curriculum

Although courses in various veterinary assistant programs vary, if the school is accredited, you can expect to learn some basic principles. You will learn basic skills to begin an entry-level position in a veterinary office, such as animal emergency medicine, laboratory procedures, and nursing methodologies. You will probably spend a lot of time focusing on small animals, as most veterinary assistants work mainly with cats, dogs, and other pets. Your courses will cover all the basics of Animal Drug Administration, disinfection and sterilization of animal cages and laboratory equipment, preparation of medical tests, and provision of routine postoperative care.

CPR and first aid are essential components of any veterinary assistant curriculum, as well as courses in the following areas:

- Animal Anatomy
- Pet care
- Asepsis techniques
- Diagnostic for images
- Clinical laboratory procedures
- Disease
- Physiology
- Office procedures
- Surgical aid and more.

These topics will prepare you for your future career. The average veterinary assistant program lasts about nine months to a year. Still, it will take longer if you go to school part-time, which may be necessary to continue working while studying.

Employment prospects and advancement opportunities for veterinary assistants

The growth in the employment of veterinary assistants has been positive in recent years and should continue to outperform many other professions. According to the Bureau of Labor Statistics, the field will increase by 21 percent through 2018. Also, there is a place to advance in these works. You will probably begin to perform basic tasks, but with merit, you can move to a higher position with more responsibility and a higher salary. It all comes down to the experience and demonstration of yourself.

If you like animals, this might be the right race for which you can opt. There are accredited veterinary assistant study programs and courses in your area, and you can begin your veterinary training soon.

VETERINARY ASSISTANTS RULE

Many people are looking for a new career. Perhaps you are preparing to finally get out of high school and are trying to figure out what you would like to do with the rest of your life. On the other hand, you may have already spent the last twenty years of your life working in a job where you feel underpaid and undervalued. Anyway, it does not matter; it needs a bright new change. You can see the work of the veterinarian.

A veterinary assistant is someone who will be there to help all types of animals and their owners. They will be there for random checks and heartbreaking diseases. Just at the moment when an animal needs another human, you, as the Veterinary Assistant, will be there to help. Of course, you might think that you are not nearly qualified for this kind of job. However, if you play your cards well and pay attention to what you are doing, you can enroll in the best education possible and be in the field of your choice in no time.

Do you have time to go to a traditional school? Even if you do, is this something you want to do? Probably not. You are going to want to make sure that you are getting your training in the best possible conditions. One of the best ways is to take online courses. With online courses, you can study your time and become a veterinary assistant before you know it. Of course, the sooner you start with the courses, the sooner you can start applying for the position.

Of all the options in Canada, many people find that choosing to become a veterinary assistant is the right choice for them. This way, you will be a part of a field that allows you to offer many options. You can work part-time, or you can work as many hours as possible. Some like to stick to an employer, while others like to allocate their available time in as many shelters and clinics as possible.

As you can easily see, there are many things you can do and accomplish as a veterinary assistant. We recommend starting online courses to see exactly what it takes to get started. This way, you will be on your way to the race of your dreams in no time!

Veterinary Technician

A veterinary technician also called an animal health technician, is trained to help veterinarians. In some countries outside North America, vet technicians are called Veterinary Nurses, and there's ongoing controversy over the utilization of the term "nurse" within the veterinary sense. Nonetheless, the term "veterinary nurses" has grown unofficial acceptance among veterinary clientele because it's an outline that they will relate to.

Vet techs need formal training and accreditation for the work, thanks to the various technical demands of this profession. Technical skills needed by the veterinary technician include, among others, venipuncture, performing skin scrapings, doing radiology procedures, hematology, microbiology, urinalysis, and serology.

Veterinary techs perform a spread of tasks, both clinical and technical, in veterinary clinics, research laboratories, animal shelters, and zoos. They assist veterinarians in doing physical examinations and help in determining the causes of illness or injury. Tasks associated with patient care include recording temperature, pulse, and respiration, dressing wounds, applying splints and other protective devices, and cleaning animals' teeth.

Administrative tasks include maintaining treatment records and conducting inventories of all pharmaceuticals, equipment, and supplies.

Vet technicians also do minor procedures like catheterizations, ear flushes, intravenous feedings, and tube feedings. In surgery, they assist the veterinarian by providing anesthesia, providing the right surgical equipment and instruments, and ensuring that the monitoring and support equipment are in good working condition.

Vet techs got to have the right training and certification for the work. They have to finish a degree in veterinary technology, which may either be a two-year associate degree or a four-year baccalaureate. These degrees are accredited by the American Veterinary Medical Association. The AVMA also accredits schools that provide online or distance education. A crucial requirement for accreditation of those learning programs is that the provision of on-the-job or volunteer hours at an animal clinic or similar facility.

After obtaining a degree in veterinary technology, the aspiring veterinary technicians got to pass credentialing examinations given by the state. Within us, the credentialing examination, called the Veterinary Technical National Exam of VTNE, is run either by a US licensing board, the state veterinary medical association, or by the state veterinary technician association. The title of the credential that a successful examinee gets will depend upon the state and, therefore, the sort of organization granting the credential. Thus, the veterinary technician could also be described as licensed (LVT or Licensed Veterinary Technician), registered (RVT), or certified (CVT). Only those that are properly certified may represent themselves as veterinary technicians and perform their required tasks in assisting the licensed veterinarian.

Aside from the initial mandatory credentialing, veterinary technicians can also enroll in advanced courses to further enhance their skills. These courses could also be within the areas of emergency and important care, anesthesiology, dentistry, small animal general medicine, large animal general medicine, cardiology, oncology, neurology, zoological medicine, equine veterinary nursing, surgery, behavior, and clinical practice. They become Veterinary Technician Specialists (VTS) upon completion of such courses.

Veterinary technology may be a fairly young profession, having officially started only within the mid-20th century. It's still struggling to realize recognition in many parts of the planet. Within us, career opportunities still increase, with a projected rise by quite 46 percent up to 2017.

WHY YOU SHOULD BECOME A VETERINARY TECHNICIAN

Becoming a veterinary technician is a perfect career option for animal lovers. In today's economy, the search for a new career can be a change of pace for those who do not have a job. In veterinarians, the technical tasks always change from day to day, the salary is competitive, and the job is to be near the animals all day! These are some of the reasons for examining the change of a professional career in the veterinary field.

As a veterinary technician, he helps keep animals healthy and happy for their owners. There are many exciting and unique tasks during the day. Sometimes they go to work in the rooms for the veterinarian, as well as from a nurse in the Office of a doctor. Other times they will be present in surgery, monitoring the patient, or helping the veterinarian with the procedure. Often, the work requires ordinary manipulation of animals during physical examinations. As you can see, a veterinary technician should vary widely day by day or even hour by hour. Different work tasks help to keep the working day interesting.

There are also many people who specialize in certain areas, for example, dentistry, surgery, and emergency medicine. Some of these people work in hospitals that provide specific services in their respective fields. But many hospitals offer everything imaginable in veterinary medicine. Therefore, it is important that a veterinary technician is well rounded in many areas, as they may be required to perform many different tasks.

In addition to the excitement of everyday life to work in a veterinary hospital, the salary of a veterinary technician helps to make them work even better. Once a person has been certified by the state in which they live, they can earn up to $ 50,000 per year, depending on the field of veterinary medicine they join. Most veterinary hospitals also on large insurance packages and pension benefits. But, that can vary from hospital to hospital. Also, note that the employment prospects of veterinary technicians are expected to increase by 35% in the next ten years! So not only will you be happy to go to work every day, you will earn a lot of money for startup!

One of the best things about the work in question is knowing that you help the animals that come to the hospital every day. There is nothing better than seeing an improvement in a sick patient or even just playing with a healthy patient who is on a routine examination. Many health experts agree that people who have pets or are close to pets live longer and look happier. Well, why not be around animals all day and make money at the same time!

Becoming a veterinary technician is one of the smartest career options you can do right now. Having an exciting job, working with animals, and being able to live comfortably are excellent reasons to look for a very exciting and meaningful career.

HOW TO BECOME A VETERINARY TECHNICIAN

Vet technologists or technicians are persons who are trained to supply assistance to veterinarians on issues like examining animals or pets physically so as to seek out the basis or causative agent of their illness or sustained an injury at a specific time. Veterinary technicians perform certain tasks like anesthesia, administering medicines, blood if necessary, and fluid.

In order to become a licensed Veterinary Technician in most countries, the person has got to undergo a minimum number of years training during a given accredited school, i.e., American Veterinary Medical Association accredited school and be awarded the associate's degree in his chosen field of distinction on successful completion in fact, while people who there have been ready to undergo with the set minimum number of years within the American Veterinary Medical Association accredited school course is going to be awarded the baccalaureate on successful completion of the complete course. It's pertinent to notice that these degrees accompany various distinctions, albeit much importance isn't attached thereto (distinction). An accredited or credentialed veterinary technician receives an in-depth education and training, which will aid him or her in understanding medical terms and also in giving adequate treatment.

In us, the AVMA is vested with the responsibility of accrediting colleges that are offering distance learning education in veterinary technology. For those that take the choice of taking a veterinary technology course through the space learning program will need to fulfill the need of acquiring some sort of clinical experience practically, before graduation so as to be a credentialed veterinary technician. This might be achieved by applying and gaining paid to add an exclusively veterinary clinic, or alternatively offering to figure for free of charge within the veterinary clinic. The Preceptors during the sensible clinical experience must be veterinarians or credentialed veterinary technicians. They're also required to instruct and log off on clinical tasks given to the scholars, then submit the records to the varsity for approval. In some cases, the tasks are videotaped and submitted to the varsity for grading. In rare cases, a rotational internship of 1-year sessions is often accessed by veterinary technology students after they need to be graduated. These special cases include large multi-specialty practices.

Acquiring knowledge in vet technology is additionally required for an individual to be credentialed. Vet technicians who are meaning to have a permit are generally required to pass certain exams before they are credentialed, and these are based upon what's required of them in their respective province or state.

Depending on the situation which the veterinary technician wants to be credentialed in, the tests could also be overseen by a state veterinary medical association, us licensing board, or the State veterinary technician association. The vet technicians are granted a specific credential that supported the person's state or governing laws in his or her place of origin or the category of the institute that's granting the credentials. These variances might be the following:

Licensure: Which is approved or permitted by a principal politician body and states that only licensed people may perform certain vet technician tasks or present themselves as vet technicians.

Registration: Which takes the method of maintaining a list of persons who were ready to meet specific requirements of being veterinary technicians but doesn't limit one from presenting oneself as a vet technician, registered or not.

Certification: this is often presented by a personal association or institute like knowledgeable body or school, and it doesn't in any way hold any legal connotation.

Achieving any of the above depends solely on the aforementioned factors.

VETERINARY TECHNICIAN COLLEGES

Any profession requires certain knowledge, skills, and training. Undoubtedly, the profession of veterinary technician also needs adequate training according to a correct veterinary technical plan. To become a truly professional veterinary technician, a person must go through two major difficulties on the way to accreditation; complete a formal academic course for two to four years, as well as cover the state-administered certification. No matter what kind of degree a person would like to obtain, an associate, or perhaps a bachelor's degree, a person should have an appropriate training plan to be adequately prepared for the future career of a veterinary technician. But at first, a student must be reliably prepared for the National Veterinary technical examination (VTNE) and subsequent employment in an animal hospital or veterinary laboratory. As a rule, the certification process is under the full control of the American Association of Veterinary councils (AAVSB).

Veterinary technical programs contain certain internship and internship opportunities in your CV. The main requirement for future Veterinary Technicians is a fundamental understanding of breastfeeding and animal treatment. Therefore, students should receive education near the laboratory and have the practical experience to be fully ready to help in all aspects of animal care, including various surgical methods.

In general, there is a standard college program of veterinary technicians that includes seven main branches of knowledge previously defined by the American Association of State Veterinary Boards (AAVSB). These are laboratory procedures, pet nursing, dentistry methods, radiology and ultrasound, pharmacy and pharmacology, surgical preparation, and help and anesthesia. Additional knowledge in Physiology, Public Health and Zoonoses will be of great help in the execution of the additional veterinary technician.

Therefore, in order to make a successful career as a veterinary technician, a person must choose a university for study. There are a variety of Colleges of veterinary technicians at high rates, both on campus and on the Internet. Today, the most chosen educational option in the field is to obtain a two-year diploma through the program of the American Veterinary Medical Association (AVMA). This program allows students to learn the main modules in animal health and welfare, physiology, management of veterinary facilities, veterinary technologies, and pet Parasitology. These modules that require practical skills are usually learned in a medical environment with the use of live animals.

The American Veterinary Medical Association (AVMA) program can be completed in two main ways (through long-term learning) - online or offline using Generally Accepted schools and universities. The universities that offer their students this program are Indiana Business School, Brown Mackie School, and Argosy College. Length education campuses like Ashworth University and Penn Foster College are really wonderful, but there are a variety of other excellent educational institutions that offer high-quality education and training.

Today, veterinary education and training have become very important for future veterinary technicians due to the rapid development of modern technology in veterinary medicine. Due to the rapid technological progress of Science in the medical industry, animal health can be improved, resulting in many employment opportunities for truly professional veterinary technicians. A person who has undergone training at the school of veterinary technicians can be employed in animal shelters, zoos, veterinary offices, and other places! Therefore, the variety of technical works is constantly growing due to advances in the technology of Veterinary Medicine. New devices and diagnostic tests are, therefore, being developed. Students who have received technical training will have an excellent opportunity to get work in one of the most developed fields today.

Therefore, if you are a person concerned about the Life, Health, and well-being of animals, you can consider the profession of a veterinary technician. But first, you will have to choose a veterinary technician from the school. Undoubtedly, after completing your training, you can become a very valuable member of a veterinary team as a veterinary technician.

VETERINARY TECHNICIAN CERTIFICATION IN CLINICAL MEDICINE AREAS

As a veterinary technician, you have the responsibility to work with the animals and provide the necessary care to keep the animals healthy. Technicians will administer first aid, take X-rays, take samples for testing, and prepare animals and instruments for surgery, among other activities. They also have the opportunity to obtain a specialized certification, if they wish. Especially for those who work in clinical medicine, the National Association of Veterinary Technicians in America (NAVTA) is an excellent resource. NAVTA has created a standard list of criteria for those interested in obtaining the status of Academy or society through the committee of Veterinary technical Specialties (CVTS).

The holdings are accessible to persons who have an existing veterinary specialty and who are interested in a specific discipline of Veterinary Medicine. To obtain academy status, students must have completed their studies and training at an accredited institution. Students must be an accredited veterinary technician to enroll in an additional certification or specialization in an Academy program.

NAVTA has approved the companies and academies listed below. However, this is not a complete list of all academies. After completing an Academy program, individuals will earn the title of the specialized veterinary technician (VTS) in the chosen discipline.

* The Academy of Internal Medicine for veterinary technicians: those are working specifically with large animal medicine, small animal medicine, neurology, and Oncology may be interested in this Academy.

* Veterinary Academy of technical anesthesia-designed for technicians who want to know more about what is involved in the treatment of anesthesia. Students will learn how to treat animals before, during, and after surgery or surgery.

* The Academy of Veterinary behavioral technicians: these people are involved in behavioral health, problem prevention, behavior modification, management, and training. Behavioral technicians often work with animals and their owners to improve the connection between the two groups.

* The Academy of veterinary surgical technicians, those who already have experience as surgical technicians,

should explore this Academy to qualify for a national exam to become a VTS (surgery).

* The Academy of veterinary technicians in clinical practice - for veterinary technicians interested in this Academy, a series of three areas will be studied: avian/exotic, canine/feline, and animal production.

Here is a list of five companies:

* Veterinary behavioral Society technicians-students of this society will learn behavioral issues such as management, modification, and training.

* The American Association of equine veterinary technicians oriented to equine veterinary technicians and other related fields, this company will discuss aspects related to the horse.

* Zoo Veterinary Technicians Association-focused on zoo animal medicine

* Emergency and Critical Care Veterinary Society: veterinary technicians working with emergency medicine and crucial surgery and veterinary care may be interested in this society. Members of this society will be informed of appropriate practices for critical patient care and other animal-related emergencies.

Persons interested in a company or Academy must first receive education and training as a veterinary technician. This can be achieved through a minimum of a two-year program from an accredited college or university. After completing a veterinary technology program, individuals must be certified, registered, or licensed, by their terms.

How to Recognize Between a Veterinary Assistant and a Veterinary Technician

You like animals, and you think a race with them might be a good idea? If so, you probably want to know the difference between a veterinary assistant and a veterinary technician. Many people expect these to be interchangeable terms, but they are wrong. There are differences in everything from education and school to earnings and career prospects.

Education and school make a difference from the beginning. Veterinary technicians have much more practical knowledge of Veterinary techniques. They are graduates of a two - year program accredited by the American Veterinary Medical Association.

Veterinary technicians also demonstrate their knowledge in order to be able to work in their conditions. After graduation, they pass the State Council exams. If they don't pass, they can't get a work permit.

Veterinary assistants don't have to worry about all this. There is no Associate Degree or two-year board review. They are usually on-the-job trained, although some have a high school education program or have obtained a non-university program certificate.

That is why the tasks of veterinary assistants are much more basic than those of an approved veterinary technician. Basically, if you are a veterinary assistant, you will do a lot of administrative tasks like filing and answering phones, a little cleaning in examination rooms and kennels, and very basic animal care tasks like keeping animals while they are being examined.

However, if you are a veterinary technician, you will make a much more practical medical care than animals. Veterinary technicians administer vaccines, perform X-rays, take and analyze samples, help during surgeries, etc.

There is a difference in the payment rate, of course. Most veterinary assistants, on average, make between $ 9-10 per hour. If you are a veterinary technician and have some years of experience, you are likely to make $ 15 or more per hour.

Which career to choose depends on how long you want to stay in the position. If you are simply looking to work with animals and need a job that does not require a diploma for part-time or temporary work, The Veterinary Assistant is the way to go. On the other hand, if you make a long-term professional choice, we recommend that you invest the time to become a veterinary technician.

Difference Between a Veterinary Assistant and a Veterinary Technician

Many people hear the terms Veterinary Assistant and veterinary technician and assume that they are interchangeable. This is incorrect. The two jobs are very different, with different responsibilities and salary scales. In fact, they require different levels of training and education.

A veterinary technician has a lot more education. In particular, he or she is a graduate of a two-year program of study that is accredited by the American Veterinary Medical Association.

That's not all. A veterinary technician is also authorized. You cannot get a license without passing a state exam. Therefore, they not only graduated from an accredited program but demonstrated through the license exam that they learned the material.

Veterinary assistants have much less training. Sometimes they have received some training in high school or have completed a certification program, but usually, they only have training in the work of their employers. They do not have a bachelor's degree, nor have they completed an accredited program of study.

For this reason, the job responsibilities of veterinary assistants are much more fundamental. They support animals during controls and clean tools and clinical areas such as kennels and examination rooms. They also do administrative work, such as filing or answering phones.

The veterinary technician, on the other hand, will perform much more complex tasks such as giving X-rays to the animals, administering vaccines, helping veterinarians in surgery, collecting and analyzing samples, to name a few.

He probably rightly assumed that the two positions do not have the same salary scale. Veterinary technicians earn a little more money and have better job prospects. They can earn $ 15 or more per hour with a few years of experience, while their average veterinary assistant earns only $ 9-10 per hour.

If you want to work with animals as a long-term career, it is better to devote time to becoming a veterinary technician. For those who just want a part-time or short-term job with little need for Education, The Veterinary Assistant is the best choice.

Similarities Between Veterinary Technicians and Veterinary Assistance

Many of those who have an interest in working with animals and in the veterinary field are often confused between the careers of a veterinary technician and a veterinary assistant. Those who wish to follow one can enroll in the other course and only discover much later that it is not the same. Although there are some similarities, there are also differences.

The similarities between these two breeds are that they both revolve around animals. Both breeds share the love and passion for animals and the desire to see the many different species without being prejudiced or having favorites. In addition to this, both also involve working with a veterinarian or animal doctor and helping in the clinic or hospital.

Compared with the similarities, there are many more differences. First, these are two completely different breeds! Secondly, they differ in education. A veterinary technician had to undergo a course of 2 to 4 years, while you do not need to have a higher education a veterinary assistant, because he has much less power and functions. In addition, these careers differ in their field of employment. As a technician, you would play the role of nurses, anesthesiologists, and laboratory and radiology technicians, not to mention what administers the Strokes and medications as well as some of the receiving jobs. On the other hand, as an assistant, it would serve as an additional set of hands around the clinic. He would not be allowed to deal with drugs and treatments, but he would be responsible for all the basic work.

In addition, these careers also differ in employment opportunities. For a veterinary technician, it would not be limited to animal clinics, hospitals, and shelters as veterinary assistants. Instead, you would be able to take jobs in zoos, biomedical faculties, and Diagnostic Research Laboratories. The options are in abundance giving an incredible amount of experiences and exposure. In addition, there is a huge difference in benefits and salaries that puts a veterinarian technician in the lead.

In short, as you can see, there are many differences between the two breeds that conclude that they are not the same. So when you sign up for a course, learn more about each career path and know which one you want.

Chapter Four

What Is an Equine Veterinarian?

Horses are special animals that have equally special temperaments. It has been said that a horse reacts easily to a rider's emotions and is very receptive to the action of its conductor, who really seems to feel what you are feeling. Being such animals, they need professionals who can treat their medical and dental conditions, ailments, and even injuries and who are knowledgeable about horses. An equine veterinarian is a doctor or surgeon who treats horse diseases and injuries and, as a human doctor, also treats and decides several moral dilemmas in horse care.

Equine Veterinarians are qualified veterinary doctors and must have passed university courses in natural sciences related to zoology, biology, chemistry, among others. In addition, they must also pass a veterinary medicine course to become doctors, preferably from a renowned school, as well as an internship in the last part of the course. After graduation, they must pass a test ordered by a regulatory body, to become licensed veterinarians and can then study again for their sub-specialty. Many Equine Veterinarians are also horse owners and enthusiasts before they become full-fledged doctors. In this work, it is important to understand the characteristics of different horses and even the peculiarities of success in this area.

Horses are very picky with people they want to do with. That is why Equine Veterinarians should really have extensive experience with different types of horses. In general, horses are classified as warm-blooded, cold-blooded, and even warm-blooded. Hot blood tends to be playful or moody, while hot blood is more relaxed and easier to carry. Equine Veterinarians are extremely talented at knowing the difference at first glance. This is very important because dealing with horses can sometimes be dangerous, especially if a horse does not feel well. You need to gain the horse's trust before starting therapy or treatment, as a horse can become aggressive or defensive in an instant.

A big part of the job of an equine veterinarian is to travel and ranch. Sometimes in a day, the doctor may have to work on up to 10 to 20 horses in a barn and may instruct ranch managers on how to properly maintain horse helmets. Other tasks performed by the equine veterinarian are surgical interventions and periodic physical examinations, vaccinations, and even dental care. Equine veterinary dentistry is a sub-specialty of Veterinary Medicine and would require at least two more years of study. In addition to the tasks mentioned above, they also help in the delivery, rehabilitation of injured horses, and even breeding excellent horse species.

If you want to be an equine veterinarian, the most important thing to consider is that you must be extremely in love with horses. In addition, it will not hurt if your family is related to horse breeding and breeding, because it takes a whole life to really understand all the features of different breeds of these beautiful creatures, and the sooner you start getting to know horses, the better. In addition, if you really like to deal with horses, the work will seem not as an obligation, but rather as a passion.

SEVERAL THINGS YOU SHOULD KNOW ABOUT AN EQUINE VETERINARIAN

There are many veterinarians working in a private bathroom. The percentage reaches 80%, and you will find 6% among them focusing on horses. This number is obtained from the Office of Labor Statistics.

When you wish or are an equine veterinarian, you must be able to accept emergency calls, conduct examinations, diagnose conditions, and provide on-site treatment under all conditions. In addition, there are many tasks you must do. One of the tasks you need to do is that your patients should be your priority. This is based on the guidelines of the American Association of Equine Practitioners. You also need to minimize the pain or fear of the Equidae you work with.

You will find that the equine veterinarian needs a lot of equipment to make the job easy. When you get this profession, you may need something to be portable. You may need a truck, van, or trailer with all the equipment inside. You can notice, treat your patients in the clinic, and you can carry your horse with the vehicle you have.

In addition, the equine veterinarian must have a good relationship with the client and the patient. This means that you must keep accurate and confidential records, wait for prescriptions, and decide for the care of Equidae when you become an equine veterinarian.

However, a diploma is the main requirement you must meet when you want to become an equine veterinarian. The degree should focus on Sciences, including Zoology, Animal Nutrition, biology, and chemistry. Then it is also necessary to complete a four-year veterinary medicinal product. In addition, you must maintain a state license that allows you to practice in the United States.

These are several things about an equine veterinarian who needs to know if he is interested in this profession. With hard work, you will be able to get the job and work with horses that need help. But you should always be careful because it can be very dangerous to work with large animals.

MOST IMPORTANT ITEMS FOR AN EQUINE FIRST AID KIT

An equine first aid kit is important to keep around all the time if you own one horse or more of them. Horses are naturally predisposed to injuries due to their active nature and can sometimes even fall with sudden illnesses that need to be treated immediately before even calling the trusted equine veterinarian. You need to make sure that the first aid kit equine must always be available, be kept in a safe and clean place, it must be complete and well-stocked with all the important elements you need to be able to treat your horse is injured or sick.

Long ropes or covers for restraint

Treating them for wounds, you should always remember that no matter how domesticated and docile they are usually, they may eventually become fiery and defensive. It is important to appease their fears by providing them with comforting and soothing words to keep them calm before starting anything. The first among the items of the equine first aid kit is the cotton rope used for moderation. This will prevent you and your horse from hurting yourself, so make sure someone gently relieves the long cotton rope around it in case your horse gets nervous.

Bandages for dressing and compression

After examining your horse and finding out that it has stable vital signs, look for injuries and fractures that may require a bandage or bandage. The most important things to include in your equine first aid kit are the gas of different sizes to cover the wounds, to be also extended gas to cover the wounds located in areas with angles that are very difficult to reach, elastic bandages to compress and stabilize the joints are inflamed, layers to provide pressure on the Bleeding notches, a lot of cottons, wide adhesive bandages to cover more space in the body as well as ribbons to fasten all of the gas and the bandages. You can use adhesive tapes and electrical tapes to hold more firmly.

Antibiotics and emergency drugs

You need to know what the normal vital signs of a horse are to determine if your friend has a fever or not. This is important because the fever manifests itself when there is an infection or a less acute condition. For example, while you treated a horse with acute injuries, a day later, you may notice that he suffers from a fever. This could mean that the wound is infected and would require a different treatment. You should also include soap, saline solution for washing wound debris, 10% Betadine solution for cleaning wide and shallow wounds, hydrogen peroxide for cleaning deeper but smaller wounds, and antibiotics in spray form, topical, and even injected into your equine first aid kit. You may also include pre-filled sedatives or painkillers prescribed by your veterinarian if you think that cleaning the wound would make your horse wild. Electrolytes should also be included in the equine first aid kit in case your horse is dehydrated, as well as baking soda.

Other items to include in your equine first aid kit

The things that you also have to keep in hand are rectal thermometer, stethoscope, a small flashlight with batteries, large size, preferably Syringes 10, 20 and 50 ml, solution in alcohol 70% to disinfect the hands, latex Gloves, clean tweezers to halt some bleeding, sponges, a knife and scissors bandage for the cut, bucket, clean, clean towels, scalpel or disposable razors, vaseline and

While you can also include other items in your equine first aid kit, they are some of the most important items to keep in stock. Also, be sure to call the equine veterinarian if you think your horse's condition is already well above your ability to provide first aid treatment.

Interest about veterinarians

Veterinary realities

With 62% of American families possessing a pet, it's a well-known fact that veterinarians are sought after. Veterinary consideration represents 14.37 billion of the aggregate sums of cash spent on Animal Care in 2013, so putting resources into an accomplished veterinarian is an unquestionable requirement for the general wellbeing and security of your four-legged companion. Veterinarians are fascinating characters, and here are some great realities about these creature murmurs.

The term veterinary originates from the Latin world veterinae, which signifies "working animals."

Mutts are the most well-known creature to show up on your veterinary assessment table, as 46.3 million families in the United States own a pooch!

Practically 80% of rehearsing veterinarians are ladies.

All veterinarians must have a claim to fame. The most widely recognized structure would be a general practice with pets and intermittent medical procedure that requires special veterinary equipment. Be that as it may, others can keep on finishing concentrated examinations in oncology, radiology, creature dentistry, dermatology, cardiology, creature Preventive Medicine, Internal Medicine or colorful medication, and little creature medical procedure.

Not all veterinarians practice medication, some work on essential innovative work of new medicines. Others, be that as it may, apply their insight into animals and use them to human issues. Veterinary Science uncovers that about 61% of all pathogens in people originate from animals. Veterinarians were additionally at the bleeding edge of jungle fever control in the United States!

Veterinarians can profit amazingly by utilizing renovated medical equipment. Since they don't treat people, they don't need to stress over the consistent improvement of new, progressively costly veterinary equipment that isn't better. They can exploit it and purchase utilized medical equipment that will assist them with lessening the expenses of visiting their pet.

Veterinarians must make a vow when they move on from medical school, promising that they will utilize their insight for the advantage and security of creature wellbeing and government assistance. Likewise, they gravely pledge to lighten the enduring of animals, to propel medical training, to elevate general welfare, and to practice their calling with pride regarding Veterinary Medical Ethics.

In certain circumstances, veterinarians can be hazardous! Regardless of how a creature carries on, its impossible to comprehend what can occur on this veterinary assessment table. Factually, the greater part of all veterinarians truly harmed in their field of work!

How to Plan for Veterinary Medical Careers

Students who love animals and are interested in the field of Health have several careers open to them. From veterinarians to firefighters, from emergency medical technicians (EMT) to veterinary assistants, there are many possibilities. Studies to become a veterinarian are like the training needed to become a male doctor. There are more than 25 universities in the United States that have a formal Veterinary Medicine training program where students can apply after graduating in biology or premedication. Participants do not need a medical degree, but still, need specific academic training and practical experience. Emergency workers can receive EMT and firefighter certifications in two years or more, depending on the level of education achieved.

Education and training

After high school, students can take their education and training to the next level. For animal doctors, they must complete a university degree and meet the admission requirements of the school of Veterinary Medicine. Most schools require students to have a cumulative weighted average of 3.0 or more and some experience working with animals. This could include volunteering, paid work, and unpaid internships.

Spend

There are several ways for students to pay for medical school. Some government programs invite medical students, including those with a career in veterinary medicine, to exchange enrollment in the form of service. For those who have maximized their government student loans and savings from university funds and need funding to get higher degrees, internships, and positions in veterinary hospital training camps, there are alternatives. Private student loans and low-interest loans from medical schools for veterinary studies can help students choose the right professional path and enter the best programs in the country, regardless of the location.

Implementation considerations

The Graduate Record Examinations (GRE) test is a preliminary step in higher education application. Most schools have a minimum acceptable score. Also considered is the personal statement on the application, like the application for obtaining the test diploma. The stakes are higher, so the answers must be well thought out and error-free. Excellent letters of recommendation from a veterinarian and other professionals are essential to the success of an admission. Above all, students must meet all deadlines for applications for admission to any program.

Job opportunities

For trained veterinarians, there are many specialties available. Opening a practice or working for someone else are two different possibilities. Many rescuers look forward to EMT being familiar with the animals in the hope of rescuing the injured animals or pairing them with rescue dogs for disaster response and recovery. If search, and rescue animals are injured, the team must have trained professionals to provide treatment. Another alternative is the Workers of the Assisted Living Institution who refer to the participants in canine therapy. The program is now common in hospitals and any health facility where patients need an emotional boost to overcome difficult times.

Veterinary Degree Opportunities

Animal Health helps a lot to provide healthy animals for families, farms, zoos, and more. The work done is highly specialized and requires a certain level of Education. Becoming a veterinarian is possible after completing a Ph.D. program from an accredited university.

Students should plan to complete a specific list of courses that will provide them with the skills needed to diagnose and treat animals. Veterinarians use their knowledge to combat disease and conduct research to understand animal health problems. The main areas of study include:

Vaccinate animals

Administering medicines to animals

Wound treatment and fracture regulation

Perform the necessary surgical intervention

Raise awareness of pet owners about caring for their pets

Before students can enter a veterinary program, they must meet certain prerequisites. Most programs require students to have at least 50 to 90 hours of completed university studies to be admitted to a doctoral program. Students who wish to become veterinarians can complete a graduate program so that they are adequately prepared for school work. University degrees can be pursued in various specialties, including biology, zoology, and Animal Sciences. These programs provide students with the necessary knowledge in the basic areas used in university studies and in the field. The work done in Physics, Statistics, Biology, and mathematics are fundamental principles that all future veterinarians must-have.

The primary program available to students is the Doctor of Veterinary Medicine. Students learn how to treat diseases and injuries in small, large, and exotic animals. The scientific bases are explored through the study of Veterinary Science. Schools emphasize students ' ability to diagnose and treat animals. Clinical courses are needed to provide students with this experience. A typical course program follows standard requirements, and students can choose a specialization such as Zoology in their third year of study. Some general courses may include:

Veterinary Microbiology

Students examine the structure of biochemistry to identify different microorganisms harmful to animals. The causes, signs, and treatments of infectious diseases are studied in relation to domestic animals.

Veterinary Anesthesiology

Medical physics and chemistry are explored to teach students how to handle anesthetics. Legal and medical procedures are learned to properly administer anesthetics to animals.

Disease

The mechanisms of how diseases occur are examined through arguments about structural and molecular catalysts. The stages of systemic pathology are discussed in the foreground of the characteristics of animal diseases.

Subjects, including the bovine procedure, pharmacology, animal nutrition, and epidemiology, join these general courses. Students should expect to receive in-depth training when working as part of a doctoral program. A degree is essential not only for basic knowledge but also for students to be successfully admitted to a curriculum.

PhD in Veterinary Medicine

Veterinarians wanting to advance their careers can do so by getting a PhD in Veterinary Medicine. The program prepares the students for different career paths, such as biomedical research, public health, human and animal health, pharmaceutical research, government service, contract research, military and academic careers.

A PhD in Veterinary Medicine is research intensive and includes clinical and academic training in addition to a science-based research specialty. The students must make their own research. Then they should write. Edit and defend their dissertation on the topic of their own choosing. This is the most important requirement for a doctorate in veterinary medicine.

Applicants for PhD program must have a bachelor's or master's degree in biology or any related subject. Other requirements include GRE scores and research experience. Applicants are also screened through an interview.

Some course subjects in a PhD program in this field include animal physical examinations, cell physiology and biology, diagnosing animals, health and disease in animals, preventive medicine, veterinary clinical rotations, veterinary anatomy and physiology, and veterinary microbiology.

Once you've earned your PhD in Veterinary Medicine, you can either work as veterinarians or as veterinary scientists. There's big demand for veterinarians and researchers across the nation.

You could go into biomedical research and play a key role in different scientific fields such as stem cell biology, transgenic animals, molecular immunology, and virology. Veterinary scientists can help make biomedical advances that are applicable to human medicine.

Veterinary scientists play a key role in public health by diagnosing outbreaks, such as Ebola virus, SARS, and West Nile Virus (among others). They can develop responses to contain the outbreak and help protect public health.

These are just some reasons why a PhD in this field is important. It gives veterinarians more training in their field while providing additional knowledge that can help them advance in their careers.

Salary Range for Veterinary Careers

The salary scale for veterinary careers varies considerably depending on many factors. Of course, your salary will be radically different depending on whether you choose a career as a veterinarian, veterinary technician, assistant veterinarian, or office manager. The salary scale will also vary depending on factors such as position, experience, merit, bonuses, commission, and profit-sharing.

A veterinarian will make the most of the money from all these professions, of course, but they also have to complete eight years of school to get a veterinary doctor. The next online is the veterinary technician, who is basically an animal nurse and must obtain at least a two-year diploma and pass a state exam. Most veterinary technicians earn a scientific partner, but there are also diploma and certificate programs in vocational schools that will qualify you for certain jobs. Some veterinary technicians also earn a science degree, which takes four years. Veterinary assistants only need to complete a certification program, which can be completed in a year or less. A director of the veterinary office does not need formal training in veterinary science, but business training and work experience with animals will help.

As a veterinarian, you can expect to earn between $ 58,726 and $ 88,170 per year, including wages, bonuses, commissions, and benefit-sharing, if any. With more experience and loyal customers, you can earn more. The salaries of veterinary technicians depend even more on experience. A veterinary technician with less than one year of experience can earn between $ 20,225 and $ 30,520, but those with 10 to 19 years of experience can earn more than $ 44,000 per year. The average salary for veterinary assistants of all skill and experience levels is between $ 21,000 and $ 32,000 per year. And as director of the veterinary office, you can expect to take home between $ 29,915 and $ 46,875 depending on experience, skills, bonuses, commissions, and benefit sharing.

There are many races in the veterinary field. He doesn't even need much education to get into this field, but if he wants to earn a higher dollar, he does.

VETERINARY TECHNICIAN SALARY

The number of salaries of veterinary technicians often does not affect a person's decision to enter the field. Love for animals and the desire to ensure their well-being are a common personality trait among those who choose to enter the veterinary discipline of Veterinary Medicine. Standards for the care and treatment of sick animals require very specific training, and once an accredited program is completed, a planned salary ranges from $ 20,000 to $ 40,000 per year. The wide range between the bottom and top of the pay scale depends on the level of education achieved and the amount of experience that the individual has in the sector. Graduate veterinary technicians can expect a higher salary scale, which usually consists of an additional $ 3000-5000 per year.

Like the health industry, Veterinary Medicine expects huge growth figures for the next few years, and most graduates will find immediate employment. While a veterinarian will perform the surgery and treat animal patients, the veterinary technician acts as an assistant in all other areas. Working as a multitasking nurse, job opportunities abound outside the obvious positions. Companies dealing with livestock, research and even pharmaceuticals need the expertise of a veterinary technician. It is in these areas that many find at the upper end of the salary of the spectrum of veterinary technicians.

As with many other fields related to medicine, veterinary technicians will spend most of their time standing. Long hours and sometimes stressful situations consider normal working hours. Occupational hazards include exposure to potentially toxic bacteria and, of course, the occasional bite of an animal. Many in the professional accept it in the framework of work and welcome it as a weight involved in helping animals in general.

Training requirements vary, but usually include a diploma or professional certification. All but a few states require that a qualification test be passed before the start of work. Many veterinarians will require it even in states that do not, as it relieves certain levels of responsibility when working with a person's pet. Certifications, specializations and level of Education will play an important role in determining your veterinary technical salary.

If you are intrigued by the ability to work with animals, and of course the reasonably competitive veterinarian technician pays the numbers, this may be the ideal area for you. Veterinary clinics offer very rewarding work, but there are many other areas that require staff veterinary technicians to monitor certain operational aspects. Education requirements are not overwhelming and, with growth and expansion expected in the coming years, job opportunities will be plentiful. Many seeking to be veterinarians find that getting certified quickly after high school and entering the field as a veterinary technician can give them an advantage when it comes to entering veterinary school at degree level. Whatever your interest in the cutting-edge levels you are expected to achieve in this area, the campaign is growing, the jobs are numerous, and the salaries are competitive. What else can be needed for a rewarding career?

What Is Necessary To Become A Professional Veterinary Surgeon?

First, let's define who a veterinarian is. In the broad sense, a veterinarian, or vet, is a physician whose primary responsibility is to prevent various animal diseases and to provide medical and surgical care to various types of animals, including farm animals, pets, zoo animals, and horses. The Royal College of Veterinary Surgeons (RCVS) is the governing body of the veterinary profession in the United Kingdom. According to the law on veterinarians adopted in 1966, only a registered veterinarian has the right to diagnose and treat injured animals and sick animals. However, there may be some minor exceptions.

Well, not everyone can become a good vet. This is a rather difficult profession that requires a number of mandatory conditions to be met. First, to become a veterinarian, a person must have a real tenderness for animals. The fact is that your entire career will be dedicated to caring for animals and interacting with them all the time. If you want to become a veterinarian only to earn high wages, do not waste your time because sooner or later, you will not endure this profession without love for animals. Sometimes a veterinarian must spend long hours helping animals. Usually, this period is fraught with many unbearable tensions for ordinary people.

Secondly, the veterinary profession requires a person a great sense of responsibility, which is extremely important for the veterinary profession, where a doctor will sometimes be required to make life or death decisions immediately. Third, to become a good veterinarian, a person must be very good at studying, especially he or she must be strong in profile scientific subjects. As far as is known, any medical profession requires a person studying to learn large amounts of information and choose the necessary material when necessary, the meaning of academic intelligence does not raise questions. Therefore, the welfare of an animal may depend on the skills and knowledge of a veterinarian who must make a correct decision on the necessary treatment that can define whether an animal will live or die.

Fourth, to master the profession of a veterinarian in the best way, a future doctor must have good communication skills. The fact is that a veterinarian has to interact with the owners of animals that are not always suitable, especially when it comes to the life of your animal. Therefore, a veterinarian may often need to comfort the owners before helping their animals. Another necessary feature for future veterinarians is curiosity. You've probably heard of situations where even the most experienced and professional doctors have no idea what's wrong with your pet. Here it is important to have a desire to look for answers, try more and more, and finally find the right treatment. This is related to love for animals. Think carefully. Do you really have enough boldness and willpower to help the animals?

Finally, an individual must have a great desire to study. It must be said that veterinary Science, like any other medical science, is certainly unlimited. You can always open something new for yourself. It is especially important for veterinarians who have the closest relationship with sick animals. While we live in a world of science and technology, new discoveries are constantly being made in the field of Medicine. Then, every year new methods of treatment are discovered, new discoveries are made, medical knowledge develops all the time rapidly. In addition, the richness of the animal kingdom constantly opens new exotic animals, whose physiology remains a secret. Therefore, not every veterinarian will be able to cope with such animals, so it is so important to constantly enrich their knowledge.

The academic sense of the future veterinarian is carefully tested during the process of applying to a course in the veterinary field. By the way, it must be said that graduation is mandatory for the registration with RCVS (The Royal College of Veterinary Surgeons). A person must obtain a degree from one of the six universities approved by the Royal College of Veterinary Surgeons (RCVS), at the Universities of Glasgow, Nottingham, Liverpool, Bristol, Cambridge, Edinburgh, and London. It must be said that the conditions of admission are quite strict, and a person will certainly have to have high academic qualifications demonstrated by the following references in his record:

- Biology "a" level, as well as one or two in Mathematics, Physics, and chemistry.

- Votes at level "a," two A and A B, or sometimes three A.

- By the way, you can pay attention to a distinction in the BTEC diploma in animal science. In addition, a person must have significant practical experience of working with animals, which is generally also considered during the process of admission to the veterinary course.

After a person has successfully completed the veterinary course and obtained the necessary diploma, he must enroll in the RCVS (The Royal College of Veterinary

Surgeons), which will give him an excellent opportunity to practice in the UK. A person is also entitled to add the letters MRCVS after his / her name, a representative member of the Royal College of Veterinary Surgeons. If a person has a desire to specialize in a field, he or she can study and receive additional diplomas in the field. The most common branches of specialization for the practice of small animals include dermatology, orthopedics, soft tissue, ear, nose, and throat. Other options may also include zoo animals, wildlife, food-producing animals, equine veterinary practice, mixed practice, research, and genetics.

So, it was just a brief summary of what the veterinary profession is like if you are not yet disappointed and have a desire to choose this route good luck! However, never forget that this ship can sometimes seem too difficult; however, remember how many animals have been treated by you and will give you more strength to go further. However, it is possible only if the profession of a veterinarian is its vocation. This is not a good choice for more people. A veterinarian must have enough strength to spend long hours serving animals and see many dead. So think carefully before making the final decision.

Kind reader,

Thank you very much. I hope you enjoyed the book.

Can I ask you a big favor?

I would be grateful if you would please take a few minutes to leave me a gold star on Amazon.

Thank you again for your support.

Anne Duval

Printed in Great Britain
by Amazon

76695024R00072